DISCARD

HOW TO BUILD A
HOUSE

Quarto is the authority on a wide range of topics.
Quarto educates, entertains, and enriches the lives of our readers—
enthusiasts and lovers of hands-on living.
www.quartoknows.com

Artwork © Martin Sodomka
Written by Saskia Lacey
Illustrated by Martin Sodomka
Edited by Heidi Fiedler
Special thanks to Ed Conner, resident foreman

6 Orchard Road, Suite 100
Lake Forest, CA 92630
quartoknows.com
Visit our blogs @quartoknows.com

MIX
Paper from
responsible sources
FSC® C017606
www.fsc.org

Printed in China
1 3 5 7 9 10 8 6 4 2

HOW TO BUILD A
HOUSE

Written by SASKIA LACEY

Illustrated by MARTIN SODOMKA

0,382

0,618

1,6

1

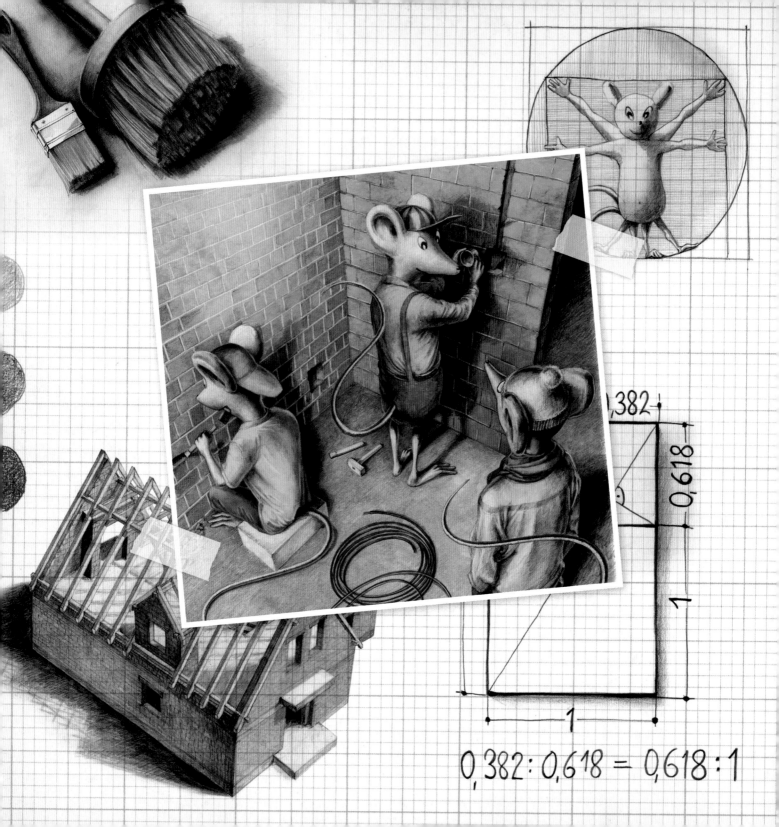

$$0{,}382 : 0{,}618 = 0{,}618 : 1$$

TABLE OF CONTENTS

MEET THE BUILDERS!

Eli
The Visionary Foreman

Ezra
The Expert on Everything

Mara
The Tenderhearted Advisor

Phoebe
The Flight Risk

Hank
The Friendly Junkyard Frog

Fritz
The Eager Workman

Luke
The Forecasting Weathermouse

Eli grinned. It was a perfect day for a cruise through the countryside.

"Now this is convertible weather!" the mouse squeaked gleefully as the wind ruffled his fur.

Driving through the dusty roads, he spotted a lovely plot of land. Eli sniffed the air. Visions of a cozy den floated through his mind. What would it be like to live in such a place?

A few adventures ago, settling down would have sounded boring. But lately, all Eli really wanted was to hole up with his band of silly friends. They had helped him succeed with each of his crazy schemes. Now the idea of building a house they could live in together tugged at the mouse's whiskers.

Step 1: The Design

When Eli pitched the house idea to his friends, Mara and Phoebe happily agreed—as long as they could help with the design.

"I'm seeing a backyard burrow, three snug bedrooms, a beautiful, cheese-filled kitchen, and windows on every wall," Mara murmured as she sketched.

"That sounds like a mansion," Phoebe said. "What we need is a simple shelter made of twigs and leaves."

"Please tell me you're not describing a nest," Eli said under his breath.

"Like a nest!" Phoebe chirped.

Eli and Mara giggled.

382

0,618

1,618

1

"Whether we're building a castle or a pigpen, we need to keep a few key ideas in mind," Mara began. "Following the principles of symmetry, scale, proportion, and rhythm will help us create an elegant design."

Phoebe bobbed her brown feathery head as Mara spoke. The bird was keen on organization. Rules were kind of her thing. "Not too shabby," Phoebe tweeted.

"Yeah, Mara," Eli exclaimed. "With your help, we'll build a mouse-tastic house!"

Blueprints

The plans architects draw for a house are called "blueprints." Blueprints show how a building will be constructed, and they can be created by hand or with a computer.

FIRST FLOOR

tool shed

garage

SECOND FLOOR

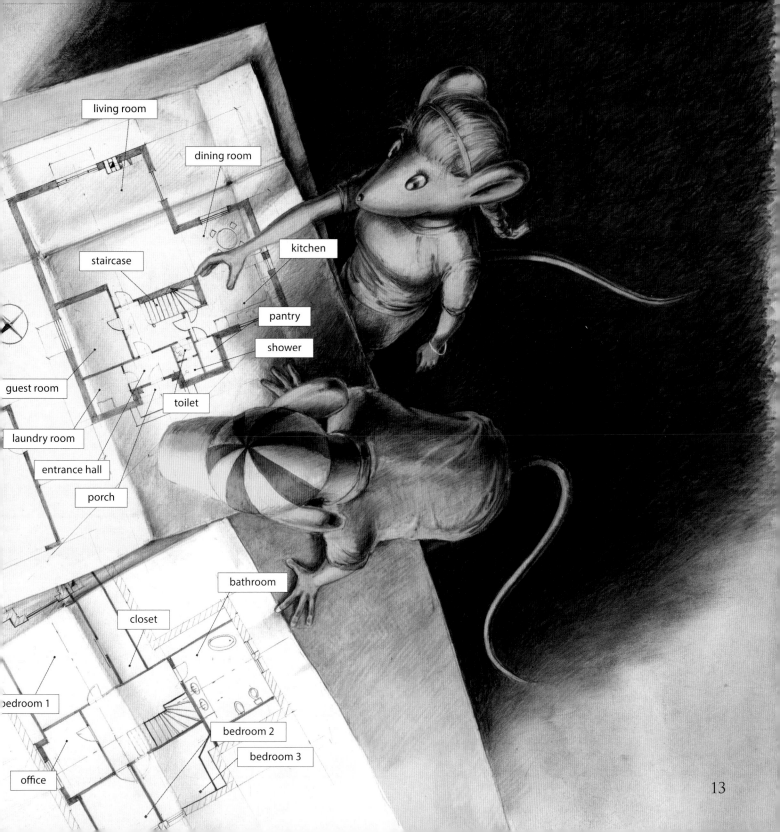

living room

dining room

staircase

kitchen

pantry

shower

guest room

toilet

laundry room

entrance hall

porch

bathroom

closet

bedroom 1

bedroom 2

bedroom 3

office

13

DESIGN PRINCIPLES

Building a house is a big project, and while creativity is important, if you want your house to look more like a home than a whirly, swirly sculpture, it's good to follow a few rules. Even free-spirited designers like Mara use these principles to guide their work.

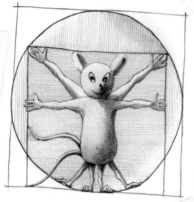

Scale

There are big houses and small houses. Eli's house will be scaled to his size. The doors must be tall enough to fit a mouse, and the knobs should be placed at paw level.

Symmetry

When the left half of the house looks the same as the right half, it's symmetrical. This house has the same number of windows on both sides. The windows are also at the same height. A symmetrical house is a sturdy house. It's also nice to look at!

Rhythm

In architecture, rhythm isn't related to music or sound. It's about the way a building looks. In the picture to the right, there are five small windows staggered over three large windows. This pattern is an example of rhythm.

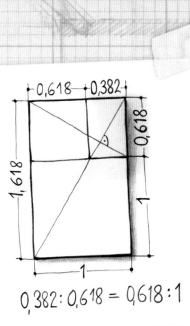

$$0.382 : 0.618 = 0.618 : 1$$

Proportions

The length and width of a room make up its dimensions. Designers avoid building rooms that are too long or too wide. Just think how tough it would be to fit furniture into a room that's 5-feet wide and 1-foot long!

"You know what's really wonderful about a house?" Mara asked with a smile.

"Besides everyone being together?" Eli asked.

"It will be a neat home base to come back to after long adventures."

"Yeah, a place to plot and plan." Eli's tail flicked excitedly. "Just think about all the inventions we'll build. It will be an idea laboratory!"

Eli couldn't wait to talk to Hank, his best frog friend and construction buddy. "Hey, pal, have you heard?" Eli called.

"About the house?" Hank's green eyebrows wiggled. "Oh, yes. I'm already thinking about what color to paint my room."

Usually Eli had to beg the frog to help with his projects. "Building a house is bigger than anything we've ever done before."

It was true. They had built a car, a plane, and a motorcycle. Difficult projects, but nothing compared to the scale of a house.

"That's what makes it exciting," Hank croaked.

"And when it's done, we'll never have to say goodbye again." Eli clapped his paws. "We'll just say good night and good morning, and go adventuring every day!"

The next day, Eli went to visit his old friend Ezra, a mechanical whiz who had once helped Eli build a motorcycle.

"Go ahead, borrow my pickup." Ezra patted the truck's hood. "She can carry over a ton. A few trips to the building site, and you're in business."

"Thanks, chum," Eli laughed.

"That reminds me." Ezra's whiskers twitched. "I might have something else you can borrow…"

"What?" Eli bounced up and down. This was going to be good.

"Oh, it's nothing." Ezra shrugged, but he was grinning. "Just a big digging excavator."

"*Aieee!*" Eli screeched. Eli *really* liked big diggers.

TRANSPORTING MATERIALS

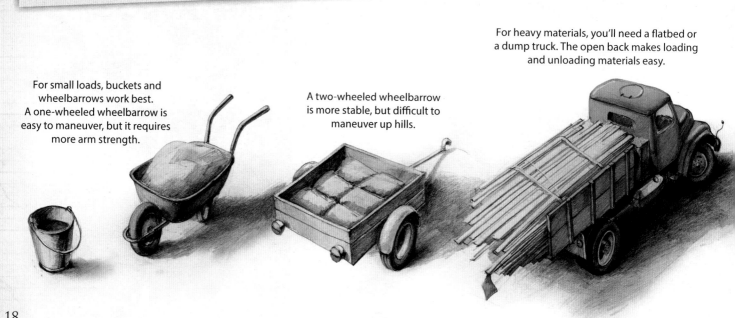

For small loads, buckets and wheelbarrows work best. A one-wheeled wheelbarrow is easy to maneuver, but it requires more arm strength.

A two-wheeled wheelbarrow is more stable, but difficult to maneuver up hills.

For heavy materials, you'll need a flatbed or a dump truck. The open back makes loading and unloading materials easy.

Dump trucks are best for moving loose material like gravel or dirt, which are then "dumped" on the ground.

Step 2: The Foundation

A week later, mice scampered back and forth across the construction site. "Project Mouse House" had begun.

"Yeah," Fritz squeaked. "It's demo day. Time to party!"

"Party?" Phoebe furrowed a feathered brow. "I thought this was serious work."

Eli squinted through the dust at the lumbering excavator. Secretly he agreed with Fritz. Was there anything better than digging big holes with a monstrous machine? *Party time, for sure*, Eli thought.

"Don't forget," Ezra called, "when we start adding the concrete strip footings, put in the usual one shovelful of cement to three shovelfuls of sand and enough water so that it's neither too wet nor too dry…otherwise, the concrete will be too weak."

"Yeah, yeah. When's it my turn on the big digger?" Eli shouted to his friend.

BUILDING THE FOUNDATION

Foundation

Many layers are needed to make the foundation of a house sturdy enough to endure all types of weather. But before a foundation can be built, the ground must be excavated. The depth of the foundation depends on the climate and the soil's condition. If the soil is sandy or loose, the foundation needs to be deeper than when building on more stable soil.

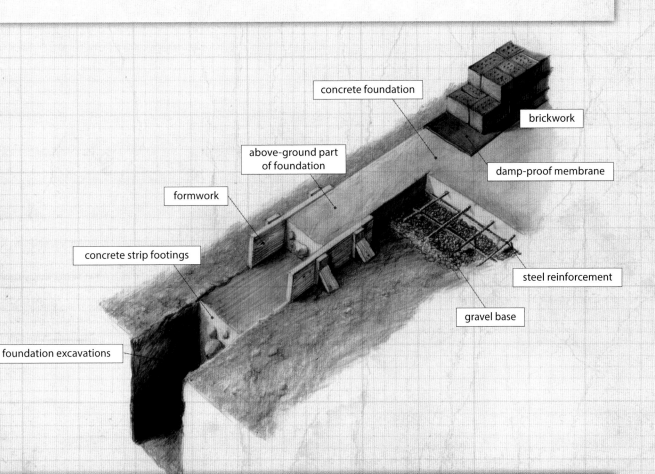

concrete foundation

brickwork

above-ground part of foundation

damp-proof membrane

formwork

concrete strip footings

steel reinforcement

gravel base

foundation excavations

Ground Materials

The words *cement* and *concrete* are often used to refer to the same thing, but concrete is actually made of water *and* cement, which binds crushed stones, sand, and rocks together. Cement is a powder, but when mixed with water, a chemical reaction occurs and allows it to harden.

23

A hand level can be used horizontally or vertically. When the bubble is centered between the two lines, the surface it's sitting on is level.

Step 3: The Walls

The crew built the walls by alternating layers of bricks and mortar. Brick by brick, the home took shape. Eli was so happy that he sang as he worked, "I'm building a house, a house for a mouse."

"A house for a mouse?" Phoebe frowned. "What about Hank and me?"

"Oh, I'm just excited, Phoebes," Eli said. "Don't worry. This house is for the whole crew."

"Seriously, Eli." The bird shivered in the cool fall air. "My own nest is soft and warm. I don't know if I belong here."

"You will, just wait," Eli protested.

But Phoebe didn't look convinced.

A plumb line is used to ensure that a vertical structure, like a wall, is level and not leaning at an angle.

24

BUILDING UP

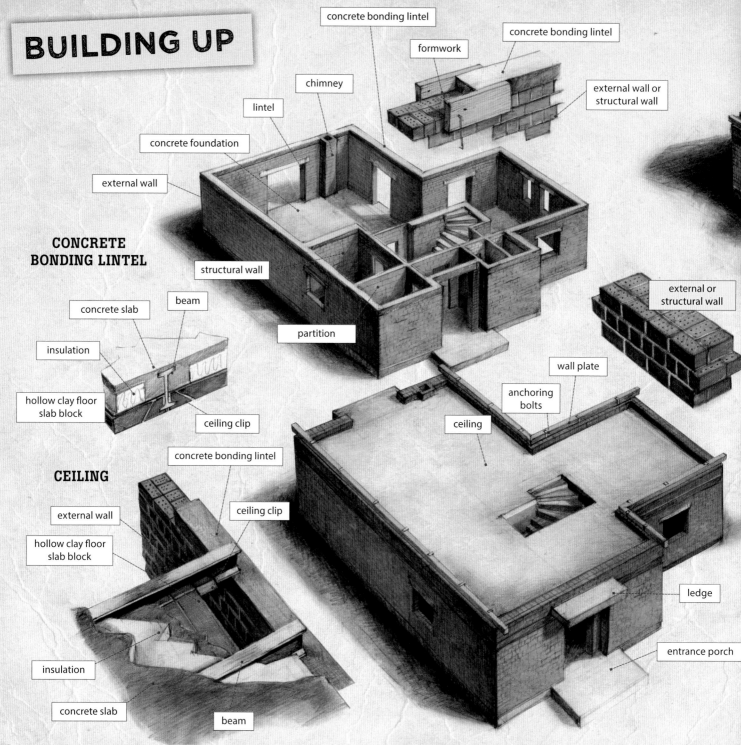

concrete bonding lintel

concrete bonding lintel

formwork

chimney

lintel

external wall or structural wall

concrete foundation

external wall

CONCRETE BONDING LINTEL

concrete slab

beam

insulation

structural wall

hollow clay floor slab block

partition

ceiling clip

external or structural wall

wall plate

anchoring bolts

ceiling

CEILING

concrete bonding lintel

external wall

ceiling clip

hollow clay floor slab block

insulation

ledge

concrete slab

beam

entrance porch

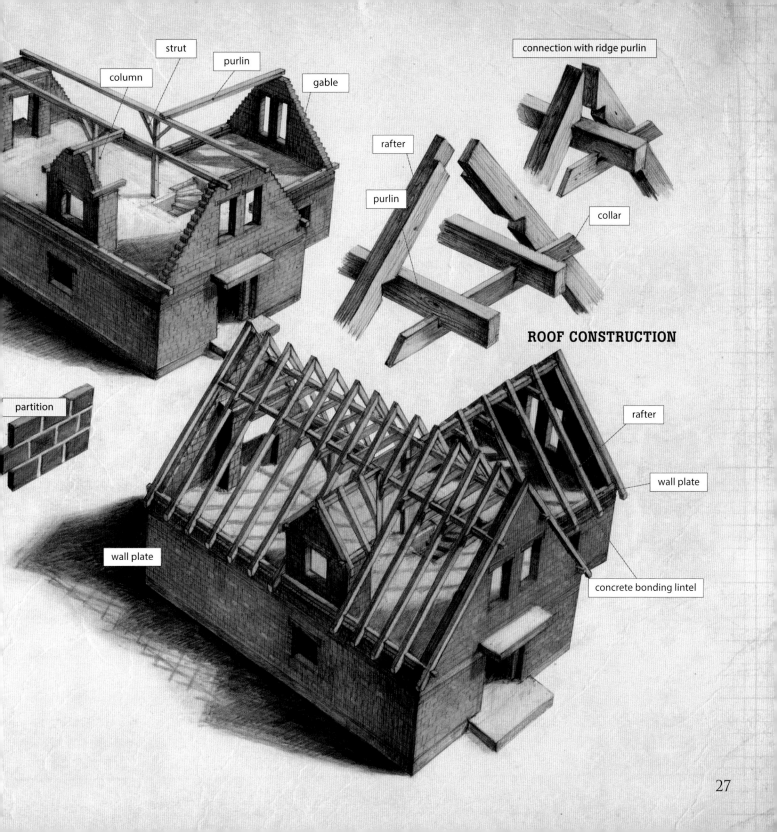

strut

column

purlin

gable

connection with ridge purlin

rafter

purlin

collar

ROOF CONSTRUCTION

partition

rafter

wall plate

wall plate

concrete bonding lintel

27

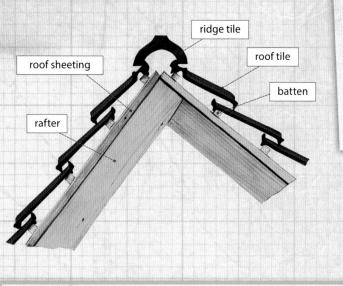

roof sheeting
ridge tile
roof tile
batten
rafter

Tiling

Proper tiling is important if you want to keep out rain. Tiles are hung in overlapping rows, starting at the bottom and working up, so rainwater doesn't get in.

three-way junction ridge tile
hip tile
roof tile
gutter

Step 4: The Roof

"Here's the next one," Luke said as he handed Eli another tile.

The crew had perfected the art of the assembly line. Hank passed a tile to Mara, who passed the tile to Fritz, who stacked the tiles up on the scaffolding next to Luke. Phoebe kept a watchful eye on the roof's construction.

"Hey, Eli," Hank called out.

"Yeah, buddy?" The mouse scampered up the roof and laid down another tile.

"Do you think all our stuff will fit in the house?" Hank asked.

Eli sighed. He was busy thinking about where to build his cheese cave.

"I don't know," Eli replied. "We can get new stuff."

"But what about—" Hank began.

"Don't worry," Eli cut his friend off. "You'll love living here!"

COVERING THE ROOF

valley

batten

counter batten

Overnight, the weather changed. The temperature dropped. Eli wound a striped scarf around his neck and fit a beanie between his ears.

"We've got to wrap up construction," Luke said. "There's a storm coming. We need a place to hole up during the cold."

Eli nodded. He was worried, but determined.
He had to finish the house so he and his friends
would have a place to spend the winter.

INSTALLING THE ELECTRICAL

Step 5: The Electrical Installation

When Phoebe and Hank didn't show up the next day, Eli fretted. Were they snowed in? The crew needed to keep working.

"Can I start cutting the chases that will hold the electrical wires?" Fritz yelped.

"I won't stop you," Eli replied. "Cutting chases is hard work. But don't make them too deep because that would weaken the wall."

"I'm on it!" Fritz cheered. The young mouse was easily excited.

"Just remember, Eli and I will be handling the wire work," Luke said sternly. "Installing an electrical system is very dangerous."

WIRING THE SOCKETS

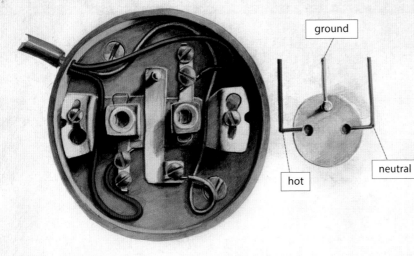

ground

hot

neutral

Electrical Outlets

There are three main wires in an electrical outlet. The hot wire carries an electrical current to the appliance. The neutral wire carries the current away from the appliance. The ground wire is for safety purposes. Remember, never attempt to take an electrical outlet apart by yourself. This job is only for professionals!

"Guys, I've got some bad news." Ezra joined the crew. "I just stopped by the garage, and I couldn't find Hank. And Phoebe's nest has a sign up that says, 'Flying south for the winter!' I think they might have bailed."

Eli was shocked. How could they not want to live in the house? The whole point of the project was to share a home with his friends!

Winter had finally arrived with a fierce snowstorm.

"We should take the day off," Luke said. "Wait for the weather to clear up. It's too cold to work in these conditions."

"I don't mind." Fritz shivered. "I'm not cold at all!"

"No, Luke's right," Eli said sadly. "We've got to stop building. I just can't believe Phoebe and Hank aren't here."

"Don't worry, my friend, they'll be back," said Luke. But Eli wasn't so sure.

"Mouse to mouse, I'm mad!" Eli griped to Mara. "Phoebe and Hank are supposed to be my best friends, but they left without even telling me."

"They *are* your friends," Mara said, patting Eli on the back. "After all, they were helping you build a house. But maybe the problem was they didn't feel at home there. Maybe they felt left out."

"Left out?" Eli was confused. "How?"

"Well, I'm sure calling it 'Project Mouse House' didn't help. And we scaled the building to mouse height. Phoebe has to fly to reach the door handles, and they're hard to turn with her beak. Plus there's no water for Hank."

"Me and my big ideas," Eli said softly. "I didn't even *think* about those things. I wanted to live with Phoebe and Hank, not chase them away. I've got to make it up to them!"

French Doors

Beautifully designed, French doors are like two large windows with hinges on opposite sides. They've been around for hundreds of years! Since there is no center support between the doors, they can be opened into or out of the room.

Eli decided to visit Ezra. His older friend always knew just what to do.

"I'm in a real bind," said Eli. "I need to make some changes to the house, and I don't know where to start."

"Is this about Phoebe and Hank?" Ezra asked.

"I was so excited about living with them, I forgot they weren't mice," Eli said. "We need to make the house more Phoebe and Hank friendly."

"Hmm." Ezra scratched his head. "I think some research is in order. I know just the place."

The two friends dashed to the town library. It was filled with books upon books! Eli didn't know there were this many books in the whole world.

"Stop gawking." Ezra nudged Eli. "Let's talk to Mr. Higgensbee."

Eli's stomach lurched. He had heard stories about the grumpy librarian.

"Excuse me, could—" Ezra began.

"Lower your voice," the librarian snapped. "This is a library." Mr. Higgensbee pointed his snout proudly in the air.

Eli couldn't help it. He laughed. He could see right up the librarian's nose.

Ezra stepped on his friend's foot. "Yes, of course," he whispered. "Where could I find books on bird and frog homes?"

"The habitat section," said Mr. Higgensbee, pointing to the back of the room.

"Thanks!" Eli squeaked loudly.

Eli and Ezra spent the day reading books about bogs and lakes, tall trees and long branches. There was so much information! But Eli wasn't sure any of the books were helping to solve his problem.

How can I make Phoebe feel at home? Eli wondered. He knew Phoebe loved to perch and think. He could find a special branch and build a nest filled with her favorite books! She had to stay then, right?

Eli still needed more ideas about how to make Hank feel comfortable. Mara and Eli decided to visit Hank's cousin, Frederick.

"Frogs are just like any other creature," Frederick explained. "They need room for the things they love. Me, I love stamps. Who knows why? But if I didn't have room for my stamps, I'd be one sad frog."

Eli thought hard. What did Hank love? He knew the frog was obsessed with cars and motorcycles, and he adored tools. That was it! Eli would gather all the tools from the construction site and build Hank a world-class workshop.

The next day, Eli was surprised to see Phoebe at the house. "I thought you flew south."

"I did," she said. Phoebe fluttered her wings shyly. "But then, I flew north. I actually missed you and your crazy ideas."

Eli smiled. "Well, we could use an extra set of wings if we're going to build the world's biggest nest."

"The world's biggest what?"

"You know, a real roost, a feather bed, a *nest!*"

Phoebe was speechless. "You don't have to do that Eli."

"Of course I do," said the mouse. "If I want my best friend to live in the same house, I need to make sure she's comfortable."

"I won't argue with that!" Phoebe chirped and flew to tell Hank the good news.

Step 6: The Bells and Whistles

The storm had finally let up. It was time to paint the house, and the team was back together! There was just one problem—they couldn't decide on a color. Phoebe was arguing for twig brown, and Fritz was begging for neon orange. Hank wanted swamp green. Eli liked primary colors like yellow, blue, and red. Mara preferred dreamy pastels.

Scaffolding

Usually made with wooden planks and metal poles, scaffolding is a temporary structure. Workers use scaffolding when they are constructing, repairing, or cleaning a tall structure.

bearer

upright

runner

coupler

scaffold boards

bracing

49

PAINTING AND DECORATING

"What have you all got against blue or red?" Eli grumbled.

"We're choosing colors for a home, not a motorcycle." Mara shook her head. "This house is our sanctuary from the wild world outside. We need soothing colors that will raise our spirits and open our hearts."

Eli thought "soothing" sounded boring, but he trusted Mara's vision. In the end, the friends decided to paint the house a beautiful pearl color.

"This color makes me feel like a truly royal rodent—and it goes with everything." Mara nodded in approval. "We can paint our own rooms whatever colors we like."

"Even neon orange?" Fritz asked quietly.

"Especially neon orange," Eli said with a smile.

Construction was wrapping up, and the water, gas, and electricity worked. The friends debated who would take the first hot shower in their big, shiny bathroom. Eli started planning a party to celebrate the new home. *We can have a BBQ,* Eli thought, *with music, food, and games!*

CENTRAL HEATING

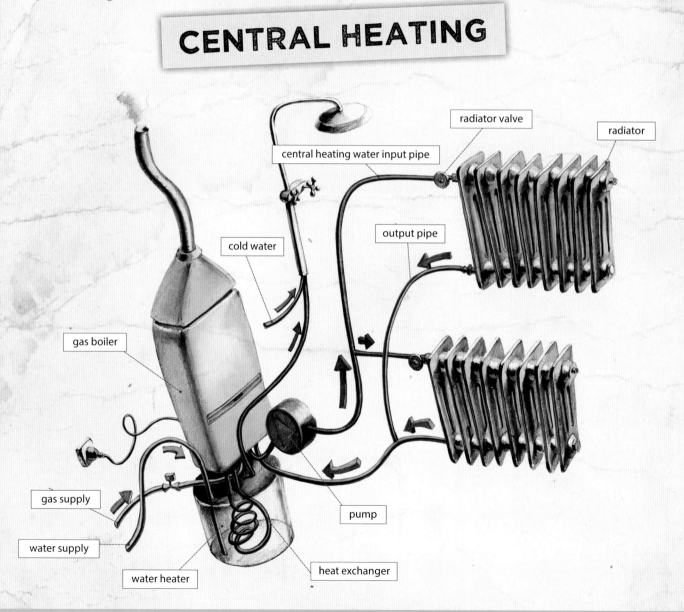

radiator valve

radiator

central heating water input pipe

cold water

output pipe

gas boiler

gas supply

water supply

pump

water heater

heat exchanger

Step 7: Celebrate!

The record player crooned a scratchy song, and a feast fit for mice, frogs, and birds welcomed Eli's friends. Could it be? The house was…finished? The animals wandered around the property, in awe of their new home.

"I can't believe we made *this*," Fritz breathed.

"Hey Phoebes, did you see your perch?" Eli grinned.

"It's wonderful, perfect, amazing!" The bird looked at her friend warmly. "Thank you so much, Eli."

"My tools!" a voice croaked loudly.

"I think Hank just found his workshop." Mara elbowed Eli.

LANDSCAPING

That spring was the happiest Eli had seen.
"I never thought I'd say this," said Eli, "but I love gardening."
Mara laughed. "I never thought you'd say that either."
"A garden makes a house feel more like home." Eli smiled. "Especially when you're surrounded by the best friends a mouse could ask for!"

56

"By the time you get back, there will be flowers," Mara said.

"Get back?" asked Eli.

"I heard Phoebe and Hank talking about a new adventure."

Eli hopped to his feet. "What kind of adventure?"

"Oh, nothing big." Mara shrugged, but her eyes twinkled with mischief. "Something about a trip around the world?"

"A. Trip. Around. The. World," Eli gasped. "Party time!"

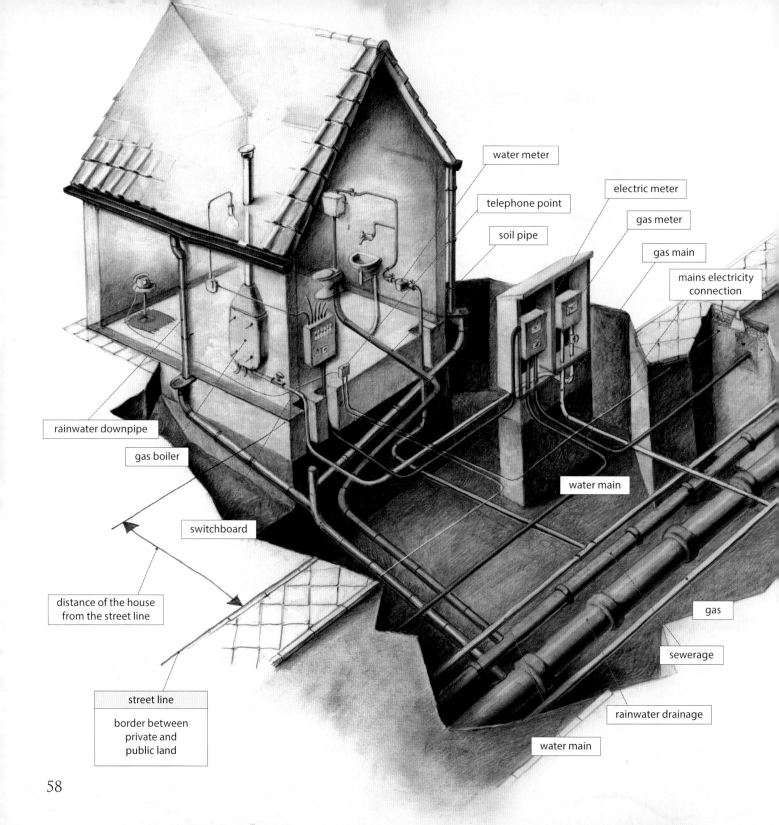

water meter

telephone point

soil pipe

electric meter

gas meter

gas main

mains electricity connection

rainwater downpipe

gas boiler

switchboard

distance of the house from the street line

water main

gas

sewerage

rainwater drainage

water main

street line

border between private and public land

58

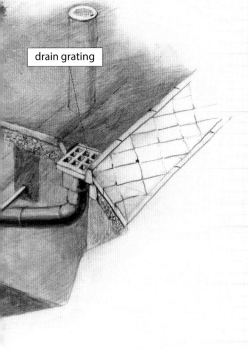

drain grating

Services

Modern life is pretty comfortable. In the past, if you needed water, you couldn't just turn on a faucet. You left the house, walked to a well, filled a bucket, and then lugged the water back to your home. And, if you wanted to read at night, you couldn't just flip a switch. You had to light a candle or an oil lamp.

Now most houses are connected to public utility services. Beneath our streets are miles of pipes, tubes, and cables that supply us with electricity, water, and gas. Every house must have instruments for measuring precisely how much energy and water it consumes. Without these instruments, our cities would not know how much to charge us for using their resources.

COLOR KEY FOR PIPEWORK

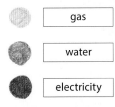

gas

water

electricity

$0.382 : 0.618 = 0.618 : 1$

Electric Meter

This device measures how much electricity is being used. We use electricity all the time. It powers our refrigerators, televisions, air conditioners, and lights. Anything you can plug in—computers, phones, toys—uses electricity.

Gas Meter

This meter measures how much gas is being used. Many things in a home require gas. If you take a hot bath or shower, gas is needed to heat the water. Gas is also used in dryers, ovens, stoves, and to warm our homes on cold days.

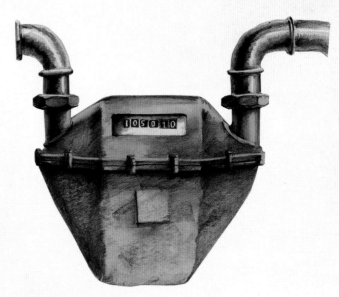

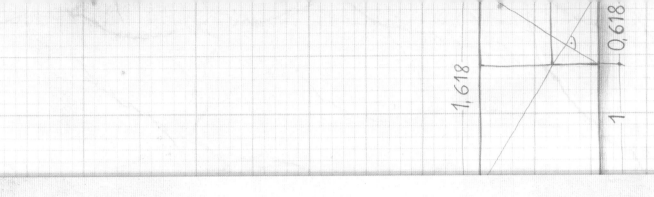

Water Meter

We use a lot of water every day. We need water to drink, cook, and clean. Dishwashers, washing machines, and sprinklers all use water. Water meters show how much of this precious liquid we use in our homes.

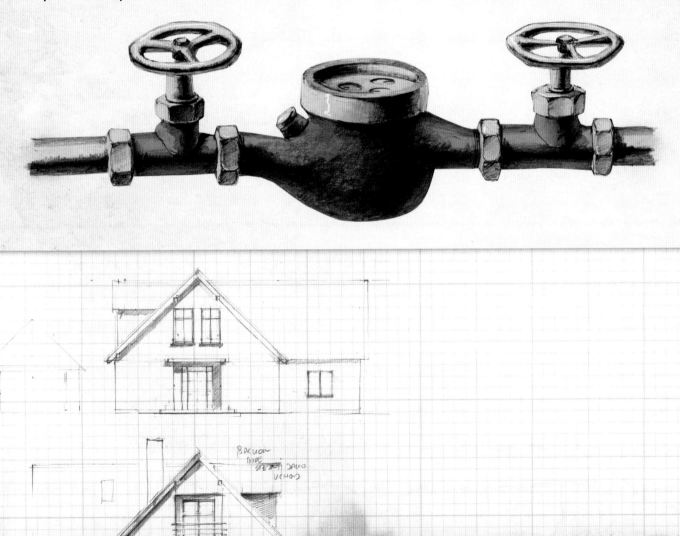

HOW TO BUILD A HOUSE IN 7 STEPS

1

THE DESIGN

Sharpen your favorite pencil. It's time to sketch the home of your dreams. The design should reflect your wants and needs. It may take a few drafts to get it right. But before you know it, you'll be breaking ground.

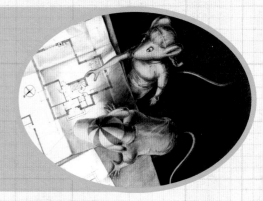

2

THE FOUNDATION

Some might think that building a foundation is as simple as pouring cement and waiting for it to dry. But you know better. Building a foundation is a process that involves excavation, laying cement, and building formwork. Phew!

3

THE WALLS

Build the exterior (outside) and interior (inside) walls. Remember to use a plumb line to make sure your walls are straight.

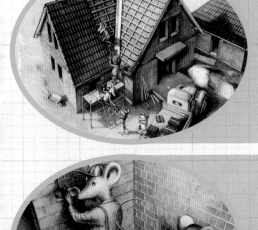

THE ROOF

Roof construction is sure to test your carpentry skills. Rafters, purlins, and collars are fitted together to create a sturdy structure. Roof tiles keep out bad weather and allow rain to slide off the house.

4

ELECTRICAL INSTALLATION

Listen to Eli. Working with wires is dangerous. Leave electrical installation to the professionals, or you might get zapped. Yikes!

5

THE BELLS AND WHISTLES

You're almost done. Sort of. You still need to plaster the walls, install the windows, and paint everything in your favorite hue.

6

CELEBRATE!

It's time to party. You've built your very own house. Break out the BBQ, and invite over all your pals!

7

HOME WITH FRIENDS

Can life be any grander?" Eli sighed happily.

"Well..." Mara hesitated.

"What is it?" Eli asked.

"It might be a little grander if someone would do his chores," Mara said.

"Chores?" Eli squinted. "What are chores?" He stifled a snicker.

Mara didn't laugh.

"Oh, all right," Eli grumbled.

"Thanks! Don't forget to clean the kitchen. It's a big ol' mess!" Mara giggled.

Eli smiled and started laughing, too. Even with chores, living at home with his best friends was even cozier than he had ever dreamed.